NW

D0605605

JUN 2 0 2007

BOOKWORMS

The Inside Story
Tepee

Dana Meachen Rau

Marshall Cavendish
Benchmark
New York

Inside a Tepee

1 cover

2 door

3 smoke flaps

4 smoke hole

5 wood poles

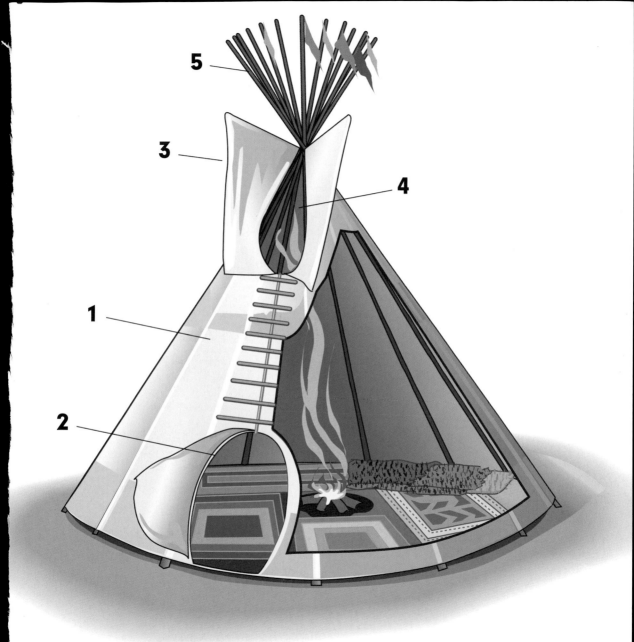

Some American Indians hunted for *buffalo*.

The buffalo moved around a lot.

The Indians needed homes they could move.

They built tepees on the *plains*.

First they put up long poles
of wood.

They set the poles in a
cone shape.

The poles made the
tepee strong.

The wind could not blow
it down.

Next they put on a cover.

The cover was made from buffalo *hides*.

They cut flaps in the hides.

This was the door.

They made a fire inside.

The fire was for cooking.

The tepee had a *smoke hole* in the top.

This hole let out the smoke.

In the winter, they closed the door flaps.

They put more hides on the tepee.

In the summer, they opened the flaps.

This kept the tepee cool.

The tepee was easy to take down.

They tied the parts to their horses.

The Indians followed the buffalo.

They set up their tepees in a new place.

Inside a Tepee

buffalo

door

fire

hides

poles   **smoke hole**

Challenge Words

buffalo (BUF-uh-low) A large, furry animal that once traveled in large herds across America.

hides The skin and fur of animals.

plains (PLANES) A large area of flat land with few trees.

smoke hole A hole inside a tepee that lets out smoke.

29

Index

Page numbers in **boldface** are illustrations.

buffalo, 4, **5**, 26, **28**
buffalo hides, 12, **13**, 20, **21**, **28**

cooking, 16
cover, 2, **3**, 12, **13**

door, 2, **3**, 14, **15**, 20, **21**

fire, 16–18, **17**, **28**
flaps, **3**, 14, **15**, 20–22, **21**, **23**, **28**

horses, 24, **25**
hunting, 4, 26

moving, 4–6, 24–26, **25**, **27**

plains, 6, **7**
poles, **3**, 8–10, **9**, **11**, **19**, **29**

setting up, 8, **9**, 12, **13**, 14, **15**, 26
smoke hole, **3**, 18, **19**, **29**
strength, 10
summer, 22, **23**

taking down, 24, **25**
tepees, 6, **7**, **11**, **27**
    cutout view, 2, **3**

wind, 10
winter, 20, **21**

About the Author

Dana Meachen Rau is an author, editor, and illustrator. A graduate of Trinity College in Hartford, Connecticut, she has written more than one hundred fifty books for children, including nonfiction, biographies, early readers, and historical fiction. She lives with her family in Burlington, Connecticut.

Reading Consultants

Nanci Vargus, Ed.D. is an Assistant Professor of Elementary Education at the University of Indianapolis.

Beth Walker Gambro received her M.S. Ed. Reading from the University of St. Francis, Joliet, Illinois.

With thanks to Nanci Vargus, Ed.D. and
Beth Walker Gambro, reading consultants

Marshall Cavendish Benchmark
Marshall Cavendish
99 White Plains Road
Tarrytown, New York 10591-9001
www.marshallcavendish.us

Library of Congress Cataloging-in-Publication Data

Rau, Dana Meachen, 1971–
Tepee / by Dana Meachen Rau.
p. cm. — (Bookworms. The inside story)
Summary: "Describes the architecture, construction, and interior
of a tepee"—Provided by publisher.
Includes index.
ISBN-13: 978-0-7614-2277-8
ISBN-10: 0-7614-2277-3
1. Indians of North America—Dwellings—Great Plains—Juvenile literature.
2. Tipis—Great Plains—Juvenile literature.
3. Indians of North America—Great Plains—Social life and customs—Juvenile literature.
I. Title. II. Series.
E98.D9R38 2006
690'.808997078—dc22
2005029851

Photo Research by Anne Burns Images

Cover Photo by Corbis/Royalty Free

The photographs in this book are used with permission and through the courtesy of:
Corbis: pp. 1, 5, 11, 28tl Tom Bean; p. 7 Richard T. Nowitz; pp. 9, 29tl Connie Ricca; pp. 17, 28bl
Phil Schermeister; p. 27 Lowell Georgia. North Wind Picture Archives: pp. 13, 15, 25, 28tr, 28br.
The Image Works: pp. 19, 29tr Eastcott Momatiuk. Getty Images: p. 21; p. 22 National Geographic.

Printed in Malaysia
1 3 5 6 4 2